Ri[...]
to [...]
Critical Writing at Bangor Unive[...] published
in a [...] of [...] nals, in[...]ding [...] Ma[...]na
and *The Rialto*. Richard has also been the recipient of two
awards. In 2011 he was awarded a place working with the
poet Paul Henry as part of the Academi mentoring programme.
In 2013, a Literature Wales New Writers' Bursary allowed him
to take a sabbatical from teaching to concentrate on
completing *Little Man*.

For Mam and Dad

Little
Man

Richard James Jones

PARTHIAN

Parthian, Cardigan SA43 1ED
www.parthianbooks.com
© Richard James Jones 2014
ISBN 978-1-909844-77-3
Edited by Alan Kellermann
Cover by www.theundercard.co.uk
Typeset by Elaine Sharples
Printed and bound by Dinefwr Press, Llandybie, Wales
The author wishes to acknowledge the award of a Writer's Bursary
from Literature Wales for the purpose of completing this collection.
Published with the financial support of the Welsh Books Council.
British Library Cataloguing in Publication Data
A cataloguing record for this book is available from the British
Library.

Exhibition note accompanying
an elegantly carved water bird:

This sculpture may be a spiritual symbol connecting the upper,
middle and lower worlds of the cosmos reached by a bird that flies
in the sky, moves on land and dives through water. Alternatively,
it may be an image of a small meal and a bag of feathers.

Ice Age Art
Arrival Of The Modern Mind
British Museum

*

Contents

*

Little Man

And with that he cut himself in two with a flurry that made the audience gasp, left his insides on show. He cracked his own ribs, removed his organs in order of least importance, kept his balls till last.

*

Snow Globe

Little man with your polymer beard and thick winter coat.
Little man with your neat stack of wood and long handled axe.
I admire how you try, little man.   I try too.

Little man...
Can we talk plainly?
One little man to another.

Have you noticed how the woodpecker never pecks?
That the needles on the trees point in the same direction.
How our fire burns without smoke.

Little man...
Do you remember the last time we were caught in a storm?
Well, there's something I need to tell you –

Old snow had flittered-up from the ground around our feet.
Flakes were drifting back through the space that holds us.
I held up my watertight palms.

Little man...
Who are we chopping this wood for?
That snow was warm, falling bone.

Washed-up

11.59pm. 4.56m.

Dogfish, dead and stinking
threaded through torn nets.

12.33am. 4.39m.

Sub-bituminous coal, a burst
burlap sack, mermaid's purse (possibly skate).

1.06am. 4.33m.

Beer bottles. No message.

...Future Proofing

Daddy's in the dressing-up box.
HONK. HONK. It's daddy clown!
WOOF. Daddy dog!

The forecast is a day of rain.
Our cardboard farmyard will be washed away,
paper cows and sheep swept off with twigs.

Daddy! Quick!
Let's build them a boat like Noah...

                                                              *

                    But wait. Now science is building the Ark.
                          We freeze heartbreaking knowledge.
                             Our first picture book is on ice –

         grey spit from the dry mouth of a neighbour's kitten
                      flaking wings of the gull and city pigeon
                           stamens from the dandelion plant.

               These are the things that will reinvent us.

*

The bread is mouldy, you see, so is the wine.
Priests have all gone south.

Scientists may try their best to save us.
But outmoded white goods still sink into the ancient pond.

The forecast remains a century of rain.

                                              *

                              In the dark times
                       will there be also singing?

                        Yes, there will be singing
                            about the dark times.
                                                Brecht

                                              *

              Who will be left to carry the tune?

                          *

                   Babies and toddlers!
              Look how they suckle and tweet
              in the bright white engine rooms!

       Already there's a new rumour going viral –
              progress has been seen wearing
           next season's wild green watercress.

                          4

This *is* a Love Poem

for Siwan

Will you meet me in the wood of unclimbed trees
bosky mist and bear traps?

Look closely at the offerings on threshold's table: words broken
open as eggshells, a carcass with an underside of brown meat
wishbones for the bleak-eyed winters.

Wild Bloom

We were led by the spittle thread of the wind
this way   that way   this way   this way   this way...

Cut flowers rotted on the kitchen table
Spiders set down eggs in the telephone receiver
Bluebottles gathered at the lip of a Whiskers tin

*

Our tongues hung, shining like wet calf's liver.
Features rippled to a coarse blur. Feet hardened
to a padded crust. Nails rooted down through
leaf-mash to marrow. Long fingers tightened
to a leathery knot. We smelt plants darken.
Heard puffballs expand. Rainwater collected
in our tracks and we drank.

The blueprint for the howl was writing itself
in our slaked throats. The canopy pulsed
as the moon beat a glass retreat. Stars shifted
into crown constellations.

We nuzzled a shoulder of moss and wild garlic.
I would salt and hang our milky hides before dawn.

What We Learn

The first time he can remember snow, the dog escaped over a collapsed fence straight under the wheels of a passing car. The sound of the last air hurrying from the dog's lungs sounded like an unfinished cheer. The driver pointed to skid marks in the ice. A neighbour said he'd write to the council about gravel – but never did.

This was how he learnt how hard it was to dig a simple hole. He asked about cremation and of the moment of his own conception – we never know when we come or go his mother told him. He remembered her exact words. On his next birthday he refused to blow out the candles on his cake.

The following winter goldfish froze to the surface of the pond. A stray cat struggled, stuck by the tongue to the ice. He rolled out a line of snow planets. Sat and recorded the slow order of melt – Mercury, Venus, Earth, Mars, Jupiter, Saturn, Uranus, Neptune, Pluto – deflating heads of buried men.

Washed-up

1.41am. 4.4m.

One gull, the eye picked clean,
missing a left wing.

2.17am. 4.52m.

Mangoes, a broken crate –
Rubens, Ripe To Perfection.

2.58am. 4.76m.

A split condom, purple and ribbed
for extra pleasure.

Sing

Be quick. Abandon your hand tools.
Gather mother and feeding son. Run.
The altar's cup is overflowing.
Offer up a dogwood fire.

Listen. The word is flashed with black.
Double bolt the chapel door. Sing.
O fryniau Caersalem ceir gweled.
For pity's sake, sing harder.

Come closer. Through metal and salt.
Hold the clean bone of our father.

Blaze

for Mathias Dixon

Candied blackberries bruise city kids.
Evening sun yawns through a tunnel.
I'm careful not to disturb the bats.

Herring gulls nest in the factory chimneys.
Mullet feed on rust from the rivets of water pipes.

*

This is our city's discarded heart.
Metal men and smelters hang like smoke rings.

*

Carthorses have been stamping.
I've come to return his belongings; black moons
of fingernails, sweat in a hammered cup.

Brickwork struggles.
Starlings dart from the furnace.

*

(It takes time for the evicted to trust us)

*

You burst into flames.
Iron filings spilled from bone.
Sparks made haloes above your head.

Let's drink together with copper tongues –
God help the sparrow and his tiny lung!

*

Look.
Ruckled smiles are packed with rhubarb and nettle.
The circus is coming to town.

*

Now, will you leave the burning furnace?

*

We can cheer the fire-eater's breath,
bathe with elephants
in the dawn sea.

Small Toes

We drift from the wooden jetty towards the quiet.
Father and baby boy, heading downstream
to the trout pools where you swam.

You are twelve years gone:
fly fishermen have long forgotten your ripple.
I've come to dip small toes into tender darkness,
bring baptism to the dead.

A new vowel sounds in the current.
Dragonflies fly off with breaking news – deep water
is binding the here, with the no-longer-here –
earlier versions of our faces, arms outstretched,
pink and yellow bathing hats.

Ok. Ok. Perhaps...

Perhaps they are the heads of fallen flowers, maybe
a reflection of pale stars, or yes! At this unlikely hour
a likely trick of cruel light.

Ten Pieces Of Advice I Should Have Listened To

1. You do not know the burn better than most. **2.** Some nights will always be too damp to burst into flames. **3.** Keep your hands off the brown flank of grazing doe. **4.** Face it: your cock and balls will end up lonely. **5.** You are not the crown jewels. Not even close. **6.** That hat is silly. **7.** Candlelight does not make you more authentic. **8.** Do not covet what's being written in your neighbour's house. **9.** The easy light the light boxes offer is not all it's cracked up to be. **10.** Always end poems structured by number on an odd digit.

Wave

So that's what dying looks like, I thought,
keeping my distance with the other visitors.
We stood while waves broke, washing up
drips and defibrillators, leaving them stranded
on the tiled floor. In a back room, doctors
put on wet suits while nurses handed out armbands
and noseclips to relatives and friends.
The water swirled at my ankles and I thought
of your sandcastle, invaded by the tide
before you went missing.

Some relatives started leaving, apologising
for forgetting their swimwear, others
said they needed coffee.
Soon it was waist-deep and nurses
with snorkels swam round checking charts
while I scanned the ward for higher ground.
Then I saw the dying

some arched, ready to dive from the ends
of their beds, others clutching lifebelts.
One climbed the walls, another choked,
prayed for Noah. In the middle, you,
shouting at a wave.

Washed-up

3.46am. 5.06m.

A bottom jaw, probably sheep.
Five teeth, no fillings.

4.41am. 5.35m.

Littmann stethoscope, drum flat
to the sand (BPM 57 and falling).

5.48am. 5.55m.

Dunlop *Green Flash*, size 42EU
little, if any, tread left.

Id and the Irrigation System

I

Desert farmers call sprinklers rainbirds.
Id loves to stand under rainbirds at night
on wet nights, when by rights
they shouldn't be whispering.
And Id shouldn't be listening.

*

Pssst Pssst Pssst

This is how they try

Pssst Pssst

And keep trying

Pssst

To tease Id to his convictions

*

This is the rainbird's call.
Time to vacate the urban sprawl.

II

Id checks-in to an expensive hotel.
Id loves the smell of cool marble in the lobby.
Gardens are lit for the keen clientele.
Id weighs up the buds from his balcony.

*

Perfumed pipes turn their delicate necks.
Rainbirds pick up their whisper.

*

Id sweats and sweats.
Shifts from foot to foot.
Id does and doesn't know where to look.

Id spreads out on the bed the way Id shouldn't be.
Rings down for a table in the Hotel's Brasserie.

Id knows how to tip.
Press a finger to the manager's lip.

III

Look at Id now! And look at those shoes!
This is Id's ideal – a bloody good meal.
Duck so perfectly pink.

The cheese board stinks.
Id sinks another drink.

*

Pssst

Come and do the can-can like only Id can

IV

How can Id resist
this secret nightshift?

Sure, Id will blame the rainbirds.
Sure, Id will blame the herd.

I can hear him now –
I'm not the first (or the last)
to charge the absurd.

V

Desert farmers call sprinklers rainbirds.
They were the first to stand under rainbirds at night.
On wet nights, when they regret ever listening.

No Good

You spoke about your father, his wandering boots,
the open chords, the way your mother breathed
when he came home.

The night you fished in the reeds, he broke,
told you he was no good. Never had been.
You were left to listen, watch the carp gulp flies.

The dog howled with your mother. Your sister
drew a stickman on the living room wall.
You put your dreams on hold.
Factory work – *it wouldn't last forever*.

You still pick up his guitar.

Len's Engineering Services

The premises of Len Beck Engineering Services in Newport
are located out of town, by the edge of the railway tracks,

and consist of a green corrugated shed surrounded by a
razor-wire fence, and I'd say, that the sets of six-inch nails

protruding in neat symmetrical rows up through the metal roof,
have the hallmarks of the handy work of Len himself.

Len actually has nothing to do with this poem.
This is a poem about Tony.

When I say Tony is a cunt, I mean *Tony Is A Cunt* is sprayed
in capital letters across the double doors of Len's shed.

I can't be certain that Tony is a cunt, because from this seat
(7A facing Swansea) I can't see the last letters of the last word.

I would in fact prefer to imagine that someone thinks Tony is a
cutie or a culinary genius. However, judging by Len's shed,

I suspect Tony is a cunt. Whatever Tony did, it must have been
pretty bad to warrant such a strong public statement

and one put down in such angry red paint. But hey-ho
we all mistakes. I could be Tony.

Ponies & Moles

As the train to Swansea slowed to halt, the conductor announced it was due to *unavoidable mechanical failures*. This was not surprising given the recent rain.

To my left, three short-legged, knackered old ponies were standing in a flooded paddock. The wooden fencing that had marked the perimeter of the land had been torn up and deposited at awkward angles tangled with the grubbed up roots of willow saplings. There was nothing to keep those creatures except water – water and their own reflections stretching out in high definition.

Arriva Trains Wales are not known for the quality of their cross-country spiritual experience. Nonetheless, it is not an overstatement to say that this delay showed me the urgency of time and certainty of rising water – it might have been the ponies' bollocks hanging in the current like clock pendulums, but the eels that spill from the river wrap themselves around all our ankles.

Had I not been watching workmen unblock the irrigation ditch, I might have seen the commotion sooner. For on the hillside slopes, magpies and crows had begun circling. Fat worms were surfacing from the tiny piles of turned earth dotted across the ground.

You see, deep under the railway tracks, and under the wet soles of the ponies' feet, blind moles had been digging. And what's more, they dug with no fear as to where they might pop up;

which, let's face it, could easily be with the bloody offcuts in the zookeeper's bucket or pinned on a board under the taxidermist's angled lamp.

Perhaps a lesson for the pony in all of us.

What Comes

I'm a flea-ridden lyric with no moon.
I'm a flea-bitten dog – no bone.

I've studied the writing on the kennel walls.
My echo barks back to an empty tin bowl.

This is it!
The last parched howl -
a doorstep plea to a freehold house
where the wet-tongued slaver and play.

Twelve weeks.
Thirteen (to be precise).
Licking paws and balls.

~

THIS POEM NEEDS A CLEAR STATEMENT

I've been working old lines in on
themselves until they mean nothing.
I worry that my mouth has wrung me dry.
That the hope of what might come won't.

~

It's true.
The clatter distracts me.

(But am I brave enough to really listen?)

To understand that the sound of hooves crossing
is the sound of my jaw dislocating -
joints dropping – spinal cord un-clicking.

Movements that plot me back.
Past the tongue and reedy mouth.

Back.
Further back.
Factory setting.

The Kidnap

Give yourself to the rakes and scarecrows
sedated at the farm's slack. To shirts left hanging
from the shady hedgerows where we slept.
Raw fields, white owlets in white flight, sweetmeats
roasting (in their skins) over an open pit. To the moon
treading water in the calf's blank stare.

Long shadows gather in muddy tunnels.
Wet tongues find me -

Who hung the deer on the barbed wire fence?
Who shook speckled eggs from the rafters?
Who burned bees from their nest?

Pine trees point needles at spent gun shells (Red. Red.).
Burning wood delivers me to the night.
Something stirs in the dried grass.

Fox? Ferret? Is that you? Vole?
Friendly bats, will you lick flies from my unblinking eye?

Things not said are hidden in our darkest barns.
We rust without realising - skeletons of a truth too late.

My mouth is stuffed with firefly, then moth.

Whiteout

Ice has melted from the fish counter.
The baker's table is not rising.
The world's whale has a snake's tongue.
Mouths gape, bone dry.

Call forth a gust of flour, Lord!
Summon maggot, fly, feather, O Lord!
Break brown bread or white.
Feed us trout, salmon, river cobbler.

Washed-up

6.43am. 5.56m.

A LifeLine tub – *Approved Animal Feed
for Ewe and Unborn Lamb*.

7.49am. 5.45m.

A red cap, *You'll Never Walk Alone*
stitched across its peak.

8.52am. 5.61m.

Dog shit (large breed).

Night Kitchen

On a shelf in the kitchen there's a tin of Colman's mustard,
a pot of damp rock salt and a black moth;
can you hear its tongue wagging?

There will be light drizzle, small teeth,
egg sacks buried in the grooves of wood.

                    On a shelf in the kitchen,
there's a herby bouquet tied with a rodent's tail, a packet
of cherry tomato seeds and peat-smoked Irish whiskey;
did you see the bottle weeping?

There will be fresh pelt, a throb of ripe clay,
sparks raised.
                    On a shelf in the kitchen,
there's a syrup tin where the wasps have fallen drowsy,
jars of whole nutmegs and stacks of tiny bones, bleached.

Have you sneaked a peek when they think we're not looking –
the moon marionettes, porcelain shrews, tinkling,
like civilised tea?

Homemakers

Slow drizzle works terrace rooftops to the shoreline.
A wet dog is barking, barking, barking
its bloody snout off. You clatter cups
in the kitchen, hunker down. Yes, weather
like this is made for tea drinking,
but lashing rain would wash the gull shit
off the stained windows.

I rearrange stems in a lean vase.
There is no refraction of light to comment on.
The wasp between bletted fruit in a copper bowl
is brittle, and I crush it, blow it into powdery flight.

Hidden in this house is a muddy well
dark with mute toads mouthing vowels.

Love Me, Love Me Not

Did you, over breakfast, at a table with soft eggs,
watch yourself eating
or in a room that needed painting, lay clothes
on the bed, as you would for a child
and as you leant to pull on your shoe, did you
find yourself holding someone else's foot?

*

You lean in on me, the weight
of the day with you. We don't know
where this is going. A man on the bench opposite
looks as if he knows something.
The ducks on the pond refuse our bread.

Spent Afternoons

I

I wake before you.
Persuasion has slipped off your lap,
is propped against pots heavy with thyme.
From the kitchen the radio
(I Can't Get No) Satisfaction.
It grows dark.

Knotweed strangles your sun lounger.
A jackdaw picks at cherry stones
shakes its head.

II

I pick blackberries from between the thorns.
The dog chases sticks too close to the edge.
We lay ourselves out, wide-eyed beneath flat skies.

My grandfather wrung the neck of an adder
on this headland, fifty years ago. His daughter
laughed as she ran barefoot through bracken.

Our fingertips are already bruised.
We stay until last light, watching the dog
search, soft-mouthed in the scrub.

Exoskeletons

Regrets pace
the submerged
engine rooms

> of storm-wrung fishing boats
> with names of lost sweethearts –
> *Gladys, Rita, May.*

Alternatives wait and wait   suspended with jellyfish.

> Here
> currents converge
> to a standstill.

Old net keeps
old hurt snagged up
with spider crabs.

Long confessions, are
long hidden

> in the blind mouths of shells –
> shells that convinced us
> (as children) of water's reach.

Displaced, salt-bitten ghosts, in shells

> like drawers of torn lists,
> spent fuses and obsolete keys.

The Day You Asked Me
Can We Really Keep The Foxes Out?

Peter talked about the risk of frost.
I covered early sweetcorn shoots with lemonade bottles,
dressed a scarecrow in my best trousers.

Tankers skirted rocks at the wide end of the bay.
Hidden wind blew gulls off Kingdom Hall's new roof.

Rain.
Pissing rain.

We hid with spider mites beneath overhanging firs.
A beehive pulsed with sorry voices.

The scarecrow hung to his splintered pole.
On the weathervane, the iron fox grinned
flashed clean teeth.

I built a makeshift coop of nailed planks and barbed wire.
We held our eyes in the gaps. You pressed against my mouth.

Acknowledgements

Thanks are due to the editors of the following publications in which some of these poems first appeared: *Poetry Wales*, *The Rialto* and *Magma*. Acknowledgement is also due to Literature Wales for the New Writer's Bursary that enabled me to complete this collection.

I am also grateful for the guidance and advice from Professor Ian Gregson, Paul Henry and Nigel Jenkins, and to Alan Kellerman for his perceptive editing and unrelenting focus on the poems.

For keeping me on my toes I'd like to thank the original JunkBox poets, Jo Furber, Adam Sillman, Jan Platt, Emily Vanderploeg, John Elcock and Zoe Gilbert – all of you have helped shape this collection.

Warmest thanks are also due to all my family, friends and colleagues for their continual encouragement and support. Finally, thank you Siwan and Hedd-Elis Jones (x).

PARTHIAN

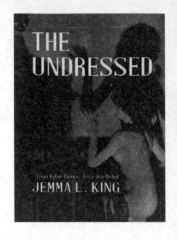

"Haunting, distinctive and sensual, *The Undressed* beautifully demonstrates King's empathy and showcases her poetic flair."
New Welsh Review

"One of the most distinctive and exciting volumes of poetry to have come out of Wales in many years" Jonathan Edwards

"The author of this powerful poetry debut... is one to watch closely ... *The Shape of a Forest* [is] both fleeting and resonant, both passionate and quiet, and I would advise you to get your hands on it." *New Welsh Review*

"A young writer of ambition and sophistication... capable of searing portraits. Here's a newcomer we should all be watching."
Robert Minhinnick

"By turns visionary and erudite... all evoked in delicate, precise lines... more than fulfils her original promise."
Samantha Wynne-Rhydderch

www.parthianbooks.com